Founding Father

By

Jesse F. Bone

AF729232

Founding Father

by Jesse F. Bone

Copyright © 2023

All Rights reserved.
No part of this publication may be reproduced, stored in a retrieval system, or transmitted in any form or by any means, electronic, mechanical, photocopying or Otherwise, without the written permission of the publisher.

The author/editor asserts the moral right to be identified as the author/editor of this work.

ISBN: 978-93-59323-61-9

Published by

DOUBLE 9 BOOKS
2/13-B, Ansari Road, Daryaganj
New Delhi - 110002
info@double9books.com
www.double9books.com
Tel. 011-40042856

This book is under public domain

ABOUT THE AUTHOR

Jesse F. Bone is a skilled and emerging author whose distinct and captivating storytelling is making ripples in the literary world. While Bone's work is not widely known in mainstream literary circles, it has earned notice for its unique perspectives, inventive storytelling, and ability to fascinate niche audiences. This author's writing style may be distinct, encompassing a wide range of genres and themes that cater to certain hobbies or literary niches. Jesse F. Bone's contributions to literature, which are frequently found among independent authors, provide readers with the opportunity to find hidden treasures and inventive storytelling outside the limitations of conventional publishing. Jesse F. Bone is a promising voice in the world of literature, with a passion for producing intriguing stories and a dedication to perfecting their craft. Their writings can span from thought-provoking fiction to intriguing non-fiction, offering readers a variety of reading experiences that might elicit emotion, provoke contemplation, or simply delight. Jesse F. Bone's literary journey as a rising author promises to deliver fresh ideas and distinctive storylines to those who enjoy the art of storytelling in all its forms. Exploring their works can lead to exciting literary discoveries as well as a respect for the different voices that enhance the literary world.

CONTENTS

CHAPTER I 7

CHAPTER II 12

CHAPTER III 20

CHAPTER IV 27

CHAPTER V 33

CHAPTER VI 40

CHAPTER VII 48

CHAPTER I

"We need data," I said as I manipulated the scanner and surveyed our little domain of rocks and vegetation. "The animate life we have collected so far is of a low order."

"There is nothing here with intelligence," Ven agreed, gesturing at the specimens in front of us. "Although they're obviously related to our race, they're quite incapable of constructing those artifacts we saw on our way down."

"Or of building electone communications or even airboats," I added.

"I expect that there is only one way to get what we want—and that's to go looking for it," Ven said as she smoothed her antennae with a primary digit. "I also expect," she added acidly, "that there might have been other places from which it wouldn't be so hard to start looking. Or did you *have* to set us down in this isolated spot?"

I glared at her and she flushed a delicate lavender. "Do you think I landed here because I *wanted* to?" I asked with some bitterness, inflating my cheek pouches to better express my disgust. "There were less than two vards of useful fuel left on the reels when I cut the drives. There isn't enough to take us across this valley. We came close to not making planetfall here at all."

"Oh," Ven said in a small voice, vocalizing as she always does when she is embarrassed. Like most females, she finds it difficult to project normally when she is under emotional stress. Afraid or angry she can blow a hole in subspace; but embarrassed, her projections are so faint that I have to strain my antennae to receive them.

Her aura turned a shamefaced nacreous lavender. I couldn't stay angry with her. She was lovely, and I was proud to be her mate. The Eugenics Council had made an unusually good match when they brought us together. The months we had spent aboard ship on our sabbatical had produced no serious personality conflicts. We fitted well, and I was more happy than any Thalassan had a right to be.

"We shall have to try other measures," I said. "Although there aren't very many natives hereabouts, we had better start looking for them rather than wait for them to look for us." I felt disappointed. I was certain that we made enough disturbance coming down for them to be here in droves, which was why I had the robots camouflage the ship to look like the surrounding rocks. There could be such a thing as too much attention.

"They could have mistaken us for a meteor," Ven said.

"Probably," I agreed. "But it would have saved a great deal of trouble if one of them had come to us." I sighed. "Oh well."

I added, "it was only a hope, at best."

"I could explore," Ven offered.

"I was about to suggest that," I said. "After all, the atmosphere is breathable although somewhat rich in oxygen, and the gravity is not too severe. It would be best to wait until dark before starting out. There may be danger. After all, this is an alien world, and Authority knows what's out there."

Her antennae dropped, her aura dimmed to gray and her integument turned a greenish black. "It doesn't sound pleasant," she said.

The sun dipped below the horizon with an indecently gaudy display of color. After the last shades of violet had faded, I opened the airlock and watched Ven, a darker blot in the darkness of the night, slip away into the shadows.

She went unarmed. I wanted her to take a blaster, but she refused, saying that she had never fired one, wouldn't know what to do with one—and that its weight would hold her back. I didn't like it. But I was unable to go with her, and it was better that she did as she wished at this time.

I sat for a while in the entrance port watching the slow wheel of the stars across the heavens, and for a moment I wished that I were a female with the rugged physique to withstand this gravity. As it was, the beauty of the night was lost on me. I breathed uncomfortably as the pressure crushed my body and made every joint and muscle ache. Males, I reflected gloomily, weren't what they were in the old days. Too much emphasis on mind, and not enough on body, had made us a sex of physical weaklings.

I wondered bitterly if a brain was as worthwhile as the Council insisted.

The next few hours were miserable. I worried about Ven, imagining a number of unpleasant things which might have happened to her. I dragged myself into the control room and fiddled with the scanners, trying the infra and ultra bands as well as the normal visible spectrum in the hopes of seeing something. And just as I was beginning to feel the twinges of genuine fear, I heard Ven.

Her projection was faint. "Help me, Eu! Help me!"

I stumbled to the entrance port, dragging a blaster with me. "Where are you?" I projected. I couldn't see her, but I could sense her presence.

"Here, Eu. Just below you. Help me. I can't make it any farther!"

Somehow I managed it. I don't know from where the strength came, but I was on the ground lifting her, pushing her onto the flat surface of the airlock—clambering up—dragging her in and closing the lock behind us. I looked down at her with pride. Who would have thought that I, a male, could lift a mature female into a ship's airlock even against normal gravity? I chuckled shakily. Strange things happen to a body when its owner is stressed and its suprarenals are stimulated.

She looked up at me. "Thank you," she said simply. But there was more behind the words than the bare bones of customary gratitude.

I helped her into the refresher and as she restored her tired body I pelted her with numerous questions.

"Did you succeed?" I asked.

"Better than I expected."

"Did you find a native?"

"Two of them." The cubicle glowed a pale green as her strength came back.

"Where?"

"Two vursts from here—down the hill. They're camped near a road. They have a big ground car with them."

"Did you see them?"

"Yes."

"What did they look like?"

The radiance in the cubicle flicked out. "They're horrible!" Ven said. "Monstrous! Four or five times our size! I never saw anything so hideous!"

"Did they see you?"

"No, I don't think so. They weren't looking in my direction at first. And I don't think they can sense, because I was frightened and they didn't respond to my projection." She was beginning to recover.

"You couldn't have been too frightened," I said. "I didn't hear you—and you can reach farther than two vursts."

"Mostly I was repelled," Ven admitted.

"Why?"

"I don't know. They smelled bad, but it was more than that. There was something about them that made my antennae lie flat against my ears.

Anyway—I did a foolish thing." The cubicle turned a pale embarrassed lavender.

"What did you do?" I demanded.

"I ran away," Ven said. "And I made a lot of noise."

"All right—all right," I said impatiently. "Go ahead and tell the rest of it."

"By the time I stopped running I was down at the bottom of the hill," Ven said. "I was dead tired—and with all that rock to climb to get back to the ship. I didn't really think I'd make it."

"But you did," I said proudly. "You're a real Thalassan—pure green."

The cubicle slowly brightened again.

"Can you find them again?" I asked.

"Of course. I wasn't lost at any time. If I hadn't panicked, I'd have been back a whole lot sooner."

"Can you go now?"

She shivered with distaste. "I can," she said, "but I don't want to."

"That's nonsense. We can't let a little physical revulsion stop us. After all, there are some pretty grim things to be seen in this universe."

"But nothing like this! I tell you, Eu, they're horrible! That's the only word that can describe them."

"Take a stat projector—" I began.

"Aren't you coming?" she asked.

"Two vursts on this planet? What do you think I am?"

Her face hardened. "I don't know," she said coldly, "but I do know this—if you don't come, I won't go."

I groaned. From her aura I could tell she meant every word. It angered me, too, because Thalassan females usually don't defy a male. "Remember," I said icily, "that you're not the only female on Thalassa."

"We're not on Thalassa," she said. Her aura was a curious leaden color, shot through with sullen red flares and blotches.

"I have no right to force you," she went on stubbornly, "but I can't handle them alone. You simply *have* to come."

"But Ven—I'm a physical cipher. This gravity flattens me. I won't mak[illegible] it."

"You will," she said. "I'll help you. But this job needs a male mind."

It was deliberate flattery, I suppose. But there was an element of truth in it. Ven obviously couldn't do it, and obviously she thought I could. I couldn't help feeling pride in her need for me. I liked the feeling. For, after all, we hadn't been mated so long that there was too great an amount of familiarity in our relationship. The Eugenics Council had taken care of that very effectively when we announced our plans for our sabbatical.

"All right—I'll go," I repeated.

With a quick light movement she touched my antennae with her primary digits. The shock ran through me clear to my pads. "You're good," she said—and the way she said it was an accolade.

CHAPTER II

"This way," Ven said, emitting a faint yellow aura that lighted the area around her. "Follow me." She staggered a little under the weight of the equipment she was carrying. I wished that we had enough power to energize an air sled—-but we had none to spare. The robots had used up most of our scanty power metal reserves in camouflaging the ship and the adaptor had taken the rest. This was going to be a miserable trip. It was going to be painful, uncomfortable and perhaps even dangerous.

It was.

We went across rocks, through sharp-twigged brush—across the saw-edged grass of the meadow below us, over more rocks, and downhill along a faint double trail that never seemed to end. I was nearly dead with weariness when Ven's aura flicked off and the dark closed in. My proprioceptors were screaming as I sank to the ground and panted the rich air of this world in and out of my aching chest.

"They're just ahead," Ven whispered. "Around that next group of rocks. Be careful."

We moved forward cautiously. "There was a fire," Ven whispered.

"There isn't now," I said. "I can't sense any heat." The night air blew a rank odor to my nostrils. My spines stiffened! I knew what Ven meant when she said that these natives repelled her. I had smelled that scent before—the scent of our ancestral enemies! So *these* were the natives, the dominant life on this planet! I gagged, my tongue thick in my throat.

"You see?" Ven asked.

I nodded. "It's pretty bad," I said.

"It reminds me of a zoo," Ven answered softly.

I nodded. It did and it was thoroughly unpleasant.

I strained my perception to its limits, pushing it through the gelid darkness, searching until I found the natives. "They're asleep," I said.

"What's that?"

"Suspension of consciousness. Something like estivation."

"Oh. Then we can approach safely?"

"If we are quiet," I replied. "Sleep is broken easily and consciousness returns quickly."

The trail deepened beyond the rocks—two rutted tracks about three vards apart. We moved forward cautiously, our senses keyed to their highest pitch. The night was oppressively still and every movement rasped loudly. My breath came fast and shallow. My heart pounded and my musk glands were actively secreting as I parted the opening to their cloth shelter, and sensed the dim forms within.

"Stat," I projected and Ven handed me the weapon. It was almost more than I could manage in my weakened condition, but I aimed it and fired a full intensity blast at the nearest lumpy figure. It jerked and flopped inside ts coverings, and the second form sat up with horrid speed!

A roar of sound came from it as the air was filled with its fetid odor. In panic I triggered a blast at the menacing figure, and it, too, flopped and laid still.

I ran my tongue over the roof of my dry mouth and called to Ven. "They're quiet now. Come in and see what we've got."

"Ugh!" Ven snorted as she entered the tent at my heels. "It stinks!"

"They're not the sweetest life form in the universe," I said as I prodded the huge mound beside me, looking for reflexes that would indicate returning consciousness.

"What are they?" Ven asked.

"Mammals," I said.

"No wonder I thought of a zoo," Ven said. "But they're so big!"

"Not on all planets," I said.

"Obviously," Ven commented. "Well—what's next? Let's get this done. I'm suffocating!"

"Hand me the probe kit," I said.

I selected two of the longest probes and made my way up to the head of the nearest monster. I scanned its braincase until I found the area I wanted and inserted the probes, driving them through the heavy bone and into the brain beneath. I clipped on the short antennae and stepped back. "Turn the control to low," I said. "Place the clips on your antennae. Now think of rising." The bulk beside me stirred and Ven gave a squeak of terror. "It's all right," I assured her. "Turn the control back to zero. This one's secure."

I went to the second and treated it like the first, and felt a justifiable pride as it reacted. Not many men could implant neuro-probes correctly on the first attempt. "All right, Ven. You can go out now. Take the controls with you. I'll see what I can do to get these brutes out of their coverings."

The tent opening swayed as Ven passed through and I bent over the nearest form. The covering was a heavy sack closed with a slide fastener much like the ones we used. I pulled and it opened, sending a flood of rank scent into the fetid air. I coughed, my eyes smarting, and found the fastener of the other sack. Retching with nausea I staggered out of the tent.

Ven sprang forward, caught me as I was about to fall, and lowered me gently to the ground.

"What are we going to do?" Ven asked as I lay panting at her feet.

"We're going to get them out of there," I said, "and take them back to the ship. I didn't come all this way for nothing." I drew one of the controls toward me, fastened the clips to my antennae, advanced the gain and thought into it. There was a stir of movement inside and a huge form came stumbling out. It stood there clad in loose cloth coverings, reeking with halogen. I looked up at the dark bulk and shivered.

"That smell!" Ven said.

"We can help it a bit," I replied and turned to the control. With its massive fore-limbs the brute ripped the cloth from its body as it moved down-wind. I made it stand and took the other control.

"Let me do it," Ven said. "You can't handle both of them in your condition."

"All right," I said, "but be careful."

"I will. Now what do I do?"

"Advance the intensity knob and think what you want it to do."

There was a flurry of movement inside the tent, the thrashing of a huge body, and the second mammal burst through the opening and staggered clumsily to a stop.

"Reduce the intensity," I said. "You're projecting too strong a stimulus. Now uncover it and send it over with the other one to cool off. They're more bearable when they're cold. They exude the scent from their skin glands to compensate for temperature."

"I know," Ven said. "I studied biology." She did as I instructed and then dropped beside me. We relaxed, gathering our strength for the climb ahead. But I didn't recover rapidly. I could move, but the exertion made me dizzy. The excitement was over and reaction had set in. "I'll never make it," I said dully.

"I can help," Ven said—"a little."

"It won't be enough. You don't have the strength to carry me." I looked at the huge bodies of the mammals gleaming pallidly in the darkness, and suddenly I had an idea. The Slaads on Valga domesticated mammals. They were quadrupedal, true enough, but they were still mammals. Why couldn't I ride one of these as they did? Those great masses of muscle should carry me easily. "I think I have a solution," I said.

"What?"

"I'll have one of them carry me."

"You can't!"

"Why not? They're controlled. And they're the only way I'll be able to get back to the ship." I picked up the nearest controller. "Let's see what happens."

Ven squeaked as the monster lifted me in the air and set me across its neck. I crossed my pads and hung on. The ground seemed terribly far away.

"How is it up there?" Ven asked.

"A little unstable," I said, "but I'll manage. Shall we go?"

We moved up the trail to the rocky abutment and turned up the hill. The brute beneath me climbed strongly and easily.

"Wait a minute," Ven said as she turned the corner behind me, "you're going too fast."

"Why don't you ride?" I called down to her. "This one moves easily enough. It's much better than walking."

"I think I will," Ven replied.

"This is all right," Ven said as we moved side by side up the hill. "The fibrils on top of its head—"

"Hair," I corrected.

"The hair of this one is longer than yours. I can hold on nicely."

The big bodies of the natives moved smoothly and powerfully, their giant strides eating up the distance we had so painfully covered some time before. Presently we came out onto the lower edge of the meadow below our ship.

Ven looked at me, her aura glowing pink with excitement. "I'll race you to the ship," she cried, and dashed off with a burst of speed.

Somehow I couldn't resist the challenge in her voice. I advanced the control knob and thought strongly. The brute jumped as though it had been whipped and leaped into a plunging run. I clung desperately for a moment and then relaxed as I caught the rhythm of the driving strides. My heart pounded, but not with fear. I had never known such exhilaration! Machines were pale compared to it. The mammal could run like a frightened skent—and it was faster than Ven's!

I caught her halfway up the meadow, and pulled away, exulting in the powerful muscles moving underneath me. I charged up to the grove of trees that concealed our camouflaged ship, and brought the mammal to a halt. It was panting, trembling, drenched with stinking sweat, but I didn't mind. I was part of it. There was a certain amount of feedback in a bipolar control circuit and I could feel the heat of its body, the beat of the great heart, the rise and fall of the broad chest, the pulse of the blood vessels in the thick neck. It was magnificent! I laughed. I had never before felt the ecstasy of physical strength!

I turned and looked back, still tasting the pleasure of the great body connected to my mind.

Ven drew up beside me. "Hai Yee!" she exclaimed. "What a sensation!"

"You liked it?" I asked.

"Liked it? *Liked* it? I loved it! Didn't you?"

"I think so," I said truthfully.

"I'm going across the meadow again," Ven said as she turned her mammal around.

"No," I said. "We have use for these two and we have no knowledge of how much they can stand. There's no sense damaging them." I frowned as I noticed the bloody scratches on the legs and body of her mammal.

Ven noted the direction of my gaze. "They're not as tough as I thought," she said with sudden contrition. "But they're not too badly damaged, are they?"

"No." I said.

I ordered the mammal to set me down. Dawn was breaking and I could see better what we had captured. They were a male and a female. On the whole, except for their mammalian ancestry, they conformed to dominant-race criteria, being erect, bipedal, predatory types with binocular vision. Their upper extremities were evolved into manipulative organs similar to our primary digits.

The most outstanding difference was the extreme sex dimorphism, which was obviously apparent in the brightening light. The physical differences were carried to such lengths that it was hard to believe that they were members of the same species.

They weren't exactly ugly, yet there was something disturbing about them. Perhaps it was the rank halogen odor of their skin glands that were still secreting despite the coolness of the air. Or perhaps it was merely that they were intelligent mammals. It was as though Authority had, in a moment of cosmic humor, drawn oversized caricatures of Thalassans and endowed them with life. I felt a subtle insult in their presence. I suppose it showed in my aura because Ven came quickly to my side.

"I told you they were disturbing," she said as we looked up at their monstrous forms towering over us.

"I'm glad they're not uncontrolled," I answered, shivering a little as I looked at them. "I suppose it's just species antipathy, but they make me uncomfortable."

"Mammals were exterminated on Thalassa long ago, weren't they?"

"Yes," I said. "They ate our eggs."

Ven walked forward and ran her primary digits over the female's legs. "They're quite well evolved," she said. "The skin hasn't a vestige of scales."

"Neither does yours except at the tip of your tail," I said tartly. "Don't get the idea that they're a primitive life form. Actually they are a *later* evolutionary type than we! If our ancestors had not developed intelligence enough to realize their peril we would be extinct—and something like them would rule Thalassa today."

Ven shivered, "How horrible! I don't like thinking about it."

"Don't," I advised.

"What are we going to do with them?" Ven asked.

"I was going to analyze them and construct a proxy, but they're far too big to duplicate with our limited resources. I suppose the only thing we can do is to insert control circuits and use them as they are."

"Won't that be painful?"

"Only psychically. Physically they shouldn't suffer a bit. The brain, you know, feels no pain. It merely interprets stimuli from elsewhere."

"In mammals too?"

I shrugged. "I suppose so. Besides, what difference does it make? Once we're through with them we can destroy them if they're too badly damaged."

"That seems unfair."

"It's not a question of fairness. It's survival. If they don't perform properly, we shall have to dispose of them or they'll be back here with a whole herd. Of course, if they operate under control, we'll turn them loose when we're through with them. I doubt that their technology is advanced enough to recognize a bio-circuit if they saw one. And if it is, they will have learned nothing new."

"But why can't we keep them—take them back to Thalassa? They'd make an unusual contribution to the Central Zoo."

"I'm afraid not," I said. "I doubt if they'd survive space. The only part of the ship large enough to hold them would be the cargo storage compartment, and that's not shielded. A hyperjump would kill them. You wouldn't want even them to die *that* way, would you?"

Her aura turned gray. "No, I suppose not."

"There isn't a chance," I said, seizing her thought before it was uttered. "It would take ten of our lifetimes to reach our nearest outpost on normal spacedrive. Forget it."

"But—"

"Come along," I said, "I'll need your help to modify these brutes."

Actually it wasn't a hard job. Their brains were well developed and nicely compartmentalized. With our probes and instruments it was a simple enough matter to implant the necessary organic extensions of our instruments.

"That should do it," I murmured as I disconnected the leads I had jury-rigged into the analyzer. "They're clean as a Fardel's tooth." I was tired, but I had the pleasant feeling of accomplishment that comes from working with organic matter. Possibly if I were not so interested in History, I'd have become a medic. I do have a certain talent along that line.

At any rate, we now had a pair of proxies. With only normal fortune they would be completely undetectable.

"Is it all done?" Ven asked as she looked over my shoulder.

"Yes," I said. "But leave the probes in place until we test them." I dragged my weary body once again into the control room and tried the headgear and circuits. They functioned absolutely perfectly.

"What do we do now?" Ven's projection came to me.

"Remove the probes and send them back to their camp. There's no sense in leaving them here."

"But Eu—"

"No," I said. "They are not toys. They're tools. They're to do a job for us. Now stop acting like a child. When they bring us metal you can play games with them—but not now. They're stressed, tired, and need rest. And they're going to get it."

"Yes, Eu." Her projection was submissive.

"But don't worry," I added kindly. "You can monitor them. I installed two extra circuits, one to the hypothalamus and the other to the tactile centers. You will be able to feel every sensation they experience. It will be just like having an extra body."

"Can I try it now?" she asked eagerly as she came into the control room.

"Go ahead," I said. "Put on a helmet and use the double control. Take them back to their camp and then neutralize the controller. As for me, I'm going to the refresher. I need it."

CHAPTER III

I awoke from partial estivation with Ven's projection vibrating my antennae. "Eu! Come quickly! They're awake!"

I groaned. What did she expect? But it might be interesting to see how they behaved. And if they panicked, someone should be there to assume control.

I checked the chronometer. I had rested for eight satts which should be enough. I felt as well as could be expected, so with only a few choice Low-Thalassic expletives to help me, I managed to clamber out of the tank and stagger into the control room. Ven already had one of the helmets on. I picked up the other and flicked the switch to "on." It was the male's—and he was talking. The words were gibberish, but the thoughts behind them were easy to read.

I was part of an entity called Donald G. Carlton, a male mammal of the human species. He was a "writer" and was mated to the female, who was called Edith and who worked in "motion pictures." They lived in a place called Hollywood, in a family unit structure faintly similar to a children's creche. Custom on this world dictated that the female take one name of her mate, which indicated that the sex was even more subservient than female Thalassans. The male's body ached, but not as badly as I would have expected. And, as I expected, there was no sensitivity in the brain.

"Hey! Edith!" Donald said. "Get up!"

"Leave me alone, Don. I'm miserable," a lighter voice answered from the lumpy sack beside him. "I had the most awful dream."

"It must be the mountain air," he replied. "I did too."

"Whatever made me think this would be fun!" Edith said. "You and your meteor-hunting!" The sack heaved and twisted and her head appeared at one end. "I feel like I've been worked over with a baseball bat. Oh! My legs!"

"You're not alone," he said. "I guess it's the hard ground and these strait-jackets they laughingly call sleeping bags."

"About that dream," Edith said. "It was horrible. There was this little green and yellow thing that looked like a cross between a lizard and a human being. It was sitting on my shoulders and I was naked—carrying it around, doing what it wanted me to do! I wanted to throw it off and stamp on it but I couldn't. I just ran and ran and all the time that little monster sat with its legs around my neck, hooting like an owl. Now, wasn't that something?"

Donald was very quiet. "You know," he said slowly, "essentially that was the same dream I had."

"But that can't be! People don't have the same nightmares."

"We did."

"Then maybe—maybe it wasn't a nightmare!"

"Nonsense. We're here. We're all right. But I think perhaps we'd better get out of here—oh, Keerist! I'm one solid bruise." He twisted around until he found the fastenings and opened the bag. With a groan he stood up.

Edith looked at him, her eyes wide with sudden terror. "Don," she said in a brittle voice, "didn't you wear pajamas when you went to bed last night?"

"Yes."

"Well, you're not wearing them now." An expression of horror crossed her face. "And neither am I," she added in a small voice.

I could feel the shock in Donald's brain as he looked down at himself. "That's not all I'm not wearing," he said dully. "I'm shaved!"

There was a brief flurry inside the other sleeping bag. "So am I!" Edith's voice was a whisper of fright. "That was no dream! I remember this. The lizard gave me something that I rubbed all over myself—and my hair came off. I didn't want to, but I couldn't help myself." Her hands went to her head and she sighed, "Well, *that's* all there. For a moment I thought—"

"My skin is different," Donald interrupted thoughtfully as he inspected himself. "It feels thicker. And I don't feel cold, although I'll bet it's nearly freezing outside."

"Don! Don't you understand? That dream was real!" Edith said.

"Of course it was,—unless *this* is a dream. We could be having a nightmare about a nightmare...."

I looked at Ven.

"Just what did you do to them?" I asked.

She glowed guiltily. "I didn't know it would take their hair off," she said. "I was worried about their scratches, and the insects were biting them. So I made them rub on some of our skin conditioner."

I raised my digits toward the sky. "There is an Authority that looks over fools and Thalassan females," I said. "What made you so sure our conditioner would work on them? It might have been poisonous."

"I tried it on the male first," Ven said.

"Genius," I breathed with icy sarcasm, "sheer genius!"

"Well," she said, "it worked!" The eternal pragmatist had applied her sole criterion. "And what's more they looked and smelled lots better after they used it."

I shrugged, gave it up and turned my attention back to the mammals.

Edith had emerged from her sack and was standing before the male.

"Do I look like a nightmare?" she demanded.

"No. More like a skinned rabbit—ouch! What did you do that for?" He rubbed his face where she struck him with her digits.

"There!" Edith said. "*Now* do you think it's a dream?"

"I never did," he replied mildly. "I've never dreamed in my life. I was just breaking it to you easy. It was real enough—even the blank spaces. I wonder—"

"You wonder what?"

"What their reason was for capturing us and then letting us go. It doesn't make sense. They wouldn't grab us just for fun. They're obviously intelligent, and probably thought we would be useful to them. But they turned us loose. So we couldn't be useful except maybe for amusement—but that doesn't jell. No. They've done something to us. They've let us go for a reason."

"Stop analyzing!" Edith said. "Why don't you just get scared, like I am!"

"I *am*," he said, "but I like to figure things out. If I know what frightens me, it doesn't bother me so much."

"Do that while we're on the way home. Get your clothes on and let's get out of here! Right away!"

"We have to pack."

"Oh, leave it! Let's get out while we can!"

"I don't think we're in any danger," he said.

"Well—I don't want to stay here a minute longer!"

"All right. We'll go. But we'll pack first. Look at it logically. They had us cold. We didn't escape. We were *let* go. So why, if they didn't want us then, should they want us now?"

"Unless they can get us any time they want us."

"You have a point there, but if that's the case, they can get us anyway. So let's pack."

"You can pack if you want to. I'm leaving!" Edith pulled the opening to the tent and slipped out.

"Edith!" Donald cried. "Wait!"

I touched Ven. "Stop her," I said.

Edith's voice came from outside. "Don!" she called in a tight voice. "Don! Help me! *I can't move!*"

"Try coming back here and see what happens," Donald said slowly.

Edith's head appeared in the entrance. "I'm back," she said in a small voice.

"I thought you would be. Now let's pack and perhaps they'll let us go. It's obvious that we can't run away."

"But why? *What's happened to us?*"

"If I told you, you'd think I'm crazy."

"Tell me anyway. It can't be any worse than this."

"I think," Donald said slowly as he began to roll up his sleeping bag, "that we were kidnapped by extraterrestrials."

"Martians?"

"Not necessarily," he said. "But if I remember my nightmare correctly, they aren't human—and they are obviously smart. So they aren't of this earth. We don't have intelligent reptiles here. And with their ability to control our actions, I'd say that they were from a considerably higher culture than ours. They've done things to us—but I don't think they did them just for fun. They want us to do something."

"What?"

"I don't know. Right now I'd guess they want us to pack our things. Let's do it and get out of here. This place smells like the reptile house in the zoo!"

I was amazed. The native's analysis was as logical as my own would have been under similar circumstances. There was nothing wrong with his mind or with his courage. That big braincase held a smoothly functioning mind and a cold courage I could almost envy. In a similar fix I wasn't sure that I could be so calm.

My respect for him mounted. If there were others like him on this world, his race could be a potential danger spot for the whole Galaxy. And, with the natural antipathy between our races, these creatures could be *trouble* if they ever reached space. I wondered for a moment if Authority had known this when It brought me here. There must be some design that I should land here when this race was still capable of being frustrated.

For the sake of civilization I would have to learn more about these mammals. Much more. But since the male had deduced so much, there was only one logical course of action. I adjusted the filters on my helmet to allow the passage of surface thoughts, twisted the dials on the controller until the meters balanced and projected gently.

"Donald—listen to me," I said.

He stiffened. "I thought you would be somewhere around," he said. "Who are you?"

"My name is Eu Kor, and I am a native of Thalassa."

"Where's that?"

"A good many spatial units from here—a good many of your light years," I amended. "I mean you no harm, but I need your cooperation. My spaceship is crippled. Our fuel has deteriorated. We need more and I want you to get it for us. We captured you because we need your help. Being a native you would not make a ripple in this society. And we would create whirlpools."

"What is this material you want?"

"A metal. Atomic number 50, a white metal used as an alloy component of primitive metallic cultures," I said. "It shouldn't be too hard to get." I didn't realize how hard it was to describe what I wanted. I wasn't getting through, and it bothered me. The culture barrier was almost as bad as though we couldn't contact mind to mind.

"I think you mean tin," he said. I grasped the concept and it seemed right.

"Bring me some and I will run tests," I said.

"And what do I get in return?"

I thought quickly. If he wanted to bargain perhaps we could reach an agreement. It's always better to have a cooperative proxy. They don't cause nearly the trouble in management. And I had other things to do than monitor natives. There was a great deal of repair work to be done on the ship before she would fly again. The subspace radio power bank had to be rebuilt and the circuits should be checked.

"I can give you knowledge that you wouldn't have for decades—maybe centuries," I said. "And I can adjust your bodies for a longer and happier life." I shot a glance at Ven still immersed in her helmet. "In fact, I have made a few adjustments already."

"So I noticed," Donald thought dryly. "Although whether they're an improvement or not I couldn't say. But did you have to go to all this trouble?"

"Think of us—and discount the fact that you carried us because our bodies are too weak for your heavy world." I said. "Did you like us?"

"No," he said. "You repelled me. I disliked you on sight, more than I can say."

"The emotion is mutual," I said. "Yet I can endure you. But with your glandular outlook you could only think of destroying us."

"That is true. But you treated us like animals."

"You are animals," I said logically.

"We are masters of this world. We recognize no higher authority. We are free people—not slaves. And unless we are treated as free agents you will get no cooperation from us."

"I can force you to do as I wish," I said.

"Prove it!"

I took over. And while Donald watched with helpless horror his hand picked up a knife and drew it across his arm. The keen edge split the tissues neatly and the blood flowed.

"Don! What are you doing!" Edith screamed and then stiffened as Ven took control.

"Observe," I said as I released control.

"Why, you—" Donald began—and then continued in a tone of wonder. "Why—the cut's closing! There's no more blood—It's gone!"

"It's just one of the improvements I mentioned," I said smugly. "You also had a patch of scar tissue on your left lung and infected kidneys. You do not have them now. Had you not met us you would have been dead within five of your years."

He was shaken. I could feel it. "I do have Bright's disease," he said thoughtfully.

"You had it," I corrected.

"All right," he said suddenly, "I'll bargain with you. You've done me a good turn and it deserves a payment. I'll help you get your metal." He grinned ruefully. "I guess I couldn't do anything else."

"It makes it easier this way," I said. I smiled to myself. I was telling him the truth, but not all of it. Nor did I trust him. There was fear and hatred in his lower centers, and a formless feeling in his upper levels that he could outsmart any damn lizard that ever lived. He didn't realize that I could read his surface thoughts.

"Just remember," I said, "I can control you completely, if necessary, and pick your brain for data whether you wish it or not. And forget those ideas of informing your authorities about us. Except with your mate you cannot communicate to anyone about us. There's a basic block in your brain that will result in irreversible mental damage if you try."

This last was not quite the truth. But I hoped that by establishing fear I would prevent talk. "Now find us samples of the metal I want." I withdrew and went back to scanning.

"What was going on there?" Edith said. "You were talking to empty air. And why did you cut yourself?"

"It was one of our reptilian friends," Don said. "Like I thought, they're right with us—every way. He's a weird sort. Wants to trade health and knowledge for tin."

"Tin?"

"Yeah. At least I think it's tin. His description of the metal fits. They use it instead of rocket juice."

"But that knife—your arm?"

"Look. No cut—no blood. That's one of the things they did to us. We've got puncture-proof skin."

"Is that good?"

"It isn't bad. And I don't think I'll ever have to shave again. As I remember I put that stuff on my face. Anyway, we now have a couple of fairy godmothers who ride around in spaceships instead of pumpkin coaches."

"You're mixing your stories," Edith said. "Cinderella travelled in the pumpkin coach, not her fairy godmother. And besides, it's not funny. We're more like those poor souls in the Middle Ages who were possessed by devils—incubuses, I think they called them."

"It makes no difference what you call them," Donald said indifferently. "Whatever they are, we've got them and they're not going to leave until they're damn good and ready. Incidentally, yours is a female, so she's probably a succubus. Now don't start screaming. You'll probably be paralyzed if you do."

"I won't scream," Edith said dully. "I'm too numb to scream."

CHAPTER IV

We had surprisingly little trouble with the two natives once they realized we could control them if we wished. Of the two, Edith was the worst. She refused to cooperate and had to be forced into the simplest actions.

"We're going to have trouble with that one," I observed as Ven looked at me with faint exasperation in her yellow eyes.

"Oh, I don't think so," she said. "Not really. This is a normal female reaction. It's a phase. Like the way I felt when the Eugenics Council selected me to be your mate."

"Did you feel like that?" I asked with surprise.

"Of course. I wanted to make my own choice."

"But you never told me."

"There was no need. I came around to the Council's view before I met you. And Edith will come around to mine. Don't worry. I know how to handle this."

And she did.

I helped a little by altering a few reflex arcs and basic attitudes, but Ven wouldn't allow me to modify the higher centers.

"There's no need to make her a mindless idiot," Ven said. "You didn't do that to Donald."

"Yes, but Donald controls his emotions. He doesn't like me any better than Edith likes you, but he doesn't work himself into an emotional homogenate every time I make a suggestion. We argue it out like rational intelligences. Often I can use his experience and viewpoint. And when I can't agree, he will cooperate rather than operate under control. He's not like that bundle of glands and emotions you are trying to make into a useful proxy."

"She *is* a problem," Ven admitted, "but if I had her here—"

"That can be arranged," I said. "I'll give you two weeks. And if that doesn't work you let me perform a prefrontal block."

"That isn't very long."

"That's all we can afford, I told her.

"All right, I can try. In a month I know I could do it."

Donald protested violently when I told him what we planned for Edith, but when I gave him the alternative, he reluctantly agreed.

He passed a story that Edith would be visiting friends, and brought her to the ship.

At once Ven went systematically to work to reduce the mammal to an acquiescent state that would permit control. Since sleep is unknown to our race but necessary for mammals, the task of breaking down the female's resistance was simplified by physical exhaustion. Ven also found that the mammal's sleeping time could be used to strengthen the new reflex channels built during her waking periods. The results were amazing, even to me, and I'm fairly well trained in neuromanipulation. Halfway through the second week the mammal's surrender was complete.

"Another day and she can go back," Ven said. "I can finish her training at long range. Now that I have the channels established, I don't think she'll be any further trouble."

I took the helmet and scanned Edith. "Hmm," I said. "Do you know what you've done? You've built yourself into an Authority image."

"I know," Ven said smugly. "She is essentially a dependent type. Her mate was her decision maker. That's why I had to get her alone. It wasn't too hard once I knew where to look. As a girl, her mother made the decisions for her. As a woman, Donald has done it. And when I faced her with situations where she had to decide and where the decisions were invariably wrong, she transferred the decision-making power to me."

I looked at her sharply. "I had no idea that you intended to make a pet out of her," I said. "Otherwise I wouldn't have permitted this."

"Well, it's too late now. And besides, it was the only way I could do it in the time you allotted. But don't worry. She'll be as good a tool as your precious Donald—maybe even a better one—because she'll do things to please me and not merely because they're expedient."

Ven had a point there. But it isn't a good policy to get emotionally involved with alien races. However, the deed was done, and as long as Ven was happy I didn't care. I only hoped that she wouldn't become too attached to the creature.

Donald was much more cooperative and much tougher. He had realized from the start that there was no profit in objecting to my demands. But, unlike Edith, he gave me no handle for leverage. He arranged his life to include the unpleasant fact of my existence, and that was that. Where Ven achieved a form of mastery, I never received anything more than acquiescence. There were levels in Donald I could not touch. At first it irked me, but then I realized that I was the greater gainer. For Donald was a constant challenge, a delight to the mind, an outward collaborator and an inward enemy. Our relationship had all the elements of an armed truce. And I often thought that if I did not have the crushing advantage of control, our contest might have been more even.

Although in time Donald's hatred became modified to a grim sort of tolerance, and his repulsion into something that closely resembled admiration, he never lost the basic species antipathy which separated us. And in that regard our feelings were mutual. The ancient Thalassan proverb that familiarity breeds friendship simply didn't apply. We held a mutual respect for each other, and in a fashion we cooperated, but I never could pierce the armor of resentment that shielded him. I tried, but finally I gave up. There would never be friendship between us. We, were too different—

And too alike.

In the days that followed the first contact, I proceeded according to approved methods of investigating alien civilizations. At my request, Donald went to the local book repository and we went through a number of works on law, government, social structure, and finance. I felt that I should have some knowledge of this mammalian culture before attempting to refuel the ship. There was no sense in calling attention to myself any more than necessary. If I could obtain what I wanted and leave quietly, I would be perfectly happy. This world was of interest—but it was too disturbing to contemplate for an extended period of time.

"You were right, Eu Kor," Ven said to me as we scanned the pattern of the mammals' culture. "If you had picked any place less isolated than this, we might have been engulfed in that maelstrom."

I nodded. "It was more luck than design," I said, "but I am happy that we are no closer. This world is not for us. It is too strange, too alien with its uncontrolled emotionalism and frightening energy."

"It reminds me of a malignant neoplasm," Ven said, "growing uncontrolled, destroying the body from which it draws sustenance. Have you ever seen such a seething flux of people—such growth—such appalling waste and carelessness?"

I shook my head. "The only parallel that comes to mind is Sennor."

"But that's a dead world—killed by a suicidal race that achieved technology before it had attained culture."

"Which is precisely the situation we have here. Or have you observed their social inequities and history? Periodically these mammals erupt in merciless riots and slaughters over things that could be settled by reason. And oddly enough, these 'wars' as humans call them have the effect of stimulating technology. This is a race that apparently loves death and battle. A barbaric horde of cultural morons, with a civilized technology geared to mutual destruction."

"Frankly, I've been scanning through Edith. I've seen only the technical excellence of their entertainment industry, and the enormous waste which goes into the making of one of their productions."

"We must have a synthesis," I said, "and pool our observations."

Ven nodded.

"I'm not at all happy about this place," I continued. "It makes me uncomfortable."

"Could we modify it?" Ven asked.

I shook my head. "It would take an entire task force to do that. Reeducation of this culture would have to begin at birth after appropriate culling. We would have to start from the beginning. I fear that the council would never authorize such an action on behalf of mammals. We are altruistic ... but not that altruistic."

"Then they will destroy themselves?"

"I fear so. This culture has a poor prognosis. But it is perhaps better so. Or would you like to see them roaming through the Galaxy?"

Ven shuddered. "Not as they are now. Not these fierce, combative stupid brutes. Individuals perhaps, but not the race. They would have to learn the rules of civilization first."

"Yet they show no sign of learning. If they can't even cooperate with their own species, how in Authority's name could they ever get along with the dissimilar races of this island universe?"

"They couldn't. We would have to quarantine them."

"So isn't it better to save the expense and let them quarantine themselves?"

"I suppose so." Ven's aura was a dull gray and mine matched the gloom of hers. It is hard to stand aloof and watch a race condemn itself to death.

We fed our observations into the analyzer, together with all extraneous data we could lay our digits on via our proxies – not to prove our conclusions but to determine the means by which we could obtain the power metal with the least possible repercussions in this society. We both realized it would be fatal to expose ourselves. The mammalian technology was sufficiently advanced for them to duplicate the essential portions of our ship, and chaos could result if they secured a road to the stars. Generations of effort would be required to confine them again to their homeworld.

Thinking in this manner caused me to take certain precautions with the drive mechanism that would ensure no trace of our craft remaining if I projected a certain impulse at a given strength. Ven, of course, was appalled at my action, although she realized its grim necessity.

And in the meantime we worked with our proxies, I attempting to establish some means of quietly obtaining the metal we needed, and Ven doing nothing so far as I could determine that would further our mission. At that, Edith was in no position to obtain metal, and Ven was too young and inexperienced in contact work to attempt a mission of such delicacy. Since Edith amused her, I was content to leave them both to their own devices while I worked with Donald to speed our departure.

"In this society," I said to Donald, "it seems that one can accomplish anything with this medium of exchange you call money."

"That's close to a fundamental truth," Donald replied.

"And you are not too well supplied with it?" I asked.

"Those four ingots I brought you last week put a vicious dent in our savings account."

"Isn't your trade as an author profitable?"

"Only in spurts. It's a feast-famine existence. But it's the only one I care to lead."

"But popular fiction makes money—and you can write."

"I wish you'd tell that to my agent. He seems to have other ideas."

"I have recently read some of your fiction," I said, "and have noticed that it has certain basics that could easily be applied to an analyzer. There is no reason why we could not cooperate and produce a work that would yield a great deal of money."

Donald laughed. "Now I've heard everything!" he said. "You mean to tell me *you* could write a book *humans* would buy?"

"No, you would write the book. I would merely furnish the idea, the research data, the plot, and the general story outline. In your popular fiction," I continued, "there are four basic elements and a plot that can be varied about twenty-five ways. There is small need for philosophy and little need for abstract thought. In fact, there is no need at all for anything but glandular excitation. All that is really necessary is plenty of action, enough understanding of the locale and events to avoid anachronism—and the basics."

"What are these basics?" Donald said. "As a writer I'd like to know them."

"There are four," I ticked them off on my digits. "First, violation of the ethical or moral code of your race; second, adequate amounts of cohabitation between the characters; third, brutality; and fourth—murderous assault."

"Hmm. Sin, sex, sadism and slaughter," Donald commented. "You know, you might have something there."

"I have prepared an outline and a synopsis of such a book," I said. "It is a historical novel. It should sell. Most historical novels do."

"You've done what?" Donald gasped. Then he laughed. "Of all the insufferable egoists I've ever seen!"

"Listen," I said, ordering him to silence while I outlined the opening chapter.

"I can't stop you," Donald said. "But why should this happen to me? Isn't it bad enough to be bossed around by you lizards without having to be forced to ghost-write your amateur literary efforts?"

"It is laid in the period of your history called the Renaissance," I continued, "and deals with a young man of a noble but impoverished house who rose to power by cleverness, amorality and skill with the sword."

"I suppose the girl is the daughter of the local duke."

"No," I said, "she is the favorite wife of a Saracen corsair."

"Well, that's a switch," Donald said. "Tell me more."

So I did. I outlined the opening and told him the major points of the whole story ... as the computer had synthesized it out of seven excellent novels of the period and a four-volume set of Renaissance history.

Donald was enthralled. "You're right," he said. "It will sell. It's lousy literature, but it's got appeal. With this story and my writing we can out-Spillane Mickey." He was more enthusiastic than I had ever seen him appear before.

"Who is Spillane?" I asked.

Donald looked at me as though he thought I was crazy and shook his head. "I can get to work on it as soon as I get home," Donald said. "And if I keep at it, it'll be ready for mailing in a couple of weeks. I'll get it off to my agent and we'll see. I hate to admit it, but I think you're right about the yarn. It should sell like hotcakes."

"That is fine. It should provide us with the medium of exchange, which is necessary in this society."

"It's not necessary," Donald grinned. "It's essential."

CHAPTER V

Donald's prediction was a good one. The book sold—and sold well. Despite the outright plagiarism of ideas and source material it was hailed as a new novel—one that stimulated thought with its realistic approach to the life of the times. And we prospered amazingly.

With the advance money, I had Donald buy the land on which the ship was resting, together with the valley and rimrock. Having thus secured our landing site I felt a bit more comfortable. The comfort was even greater when, at Donald's suggestion, a fence was placed around the property and electronic tell-tales were installed. The remainder of the royalties were used to purchase tin and supplies.

But despite our prosperity and the regular supply of tin that came to me as a result of my adventure in fiction, and the certainty that Ven and I would be leaving, Donald was not happy.

As a successful new author he had to travel to meetings in various cities. He had to speak at public gatherings. He had to meet with publishers eager to receive rights to his next book. And Edith did not go with him.

Ven was adamant on this point. "It's bad enough that she is working on this motion picture," she said, "but I'm not going to have her traveling all over the face of this planet. She's the only amusement I have since we must stay cooped up in this place. I'm not going to let her go."

Donald was upset about it. He was so angry that he came to visit me voluntarily, and the sight of Edith's little car parked under the trees below the ship infuriated him even more. It took the controller to make him keep his distance as he stood in front of the airlock and hated me.

"Damn you!" he swore. "You can't do this to me! Edith's my wife and I don't like this relationship between her and that—that *dinosaur*! It isn't healthy."

"It's out of my hands," I said. "Edith is Ven's responsibility."

"It's not only that," he raged. "Ever since you lizards butted into our lives Edith looks at me like I was a stranger." His face twisted. "I'll admit she has her reasons. But that gives her no call to ask Ven's advice rather than mine. When I told her I wanted her to come with me, the first thing she said was that she'd ask Ven. She doesn't do one damn thing without that cold-blooded little monster's consent! She even asks advice on what clothes she should wear!" He laughed harshly. "The blind asking advice from the blind!"

I couldn't help chuckling. Ven, like all Thalassans, had never worn anything in her life except a utility belt. Clothing has never been a feature of our culture. Since it isn't necessary on Thalassa, it was never developed, and since our sex impulses are periodic it has never been useful to attract either males or females. "I can see your point," I said. "Ven's ideas along that line would be zero."

"Not quite," Donald said angrily. "She likes moccasins. Apparently they make feet look more like your pads."

"Well?"

"But that's it! Edith's idea of what a well-dressed housewife should wear is—*moccasins*! She damn near caused a riot the other day when our TV repairman called to fix the set. We'll be lucky if we're not forced to move because of that little incident!"

"I'll speak to Ven," I said. "And if that doesn't work, I'll insert a block against such a thing happening again. I don't want special attention called to you. That sort of thing will stop right now."

"Thanks," Donald said. "But I should be the one to stop it."

"Face it," I replied, "you aren't. Not now. But you will be once we're gone."

"Which can't be too soon to suit me," he said. "I spend every spare moment collecting tin for you. Edie doesn't. She *wants* Ven to stay."

"They seem to be happy with each other. Edith comes up here regularly."

"I know," he said bitterly. "She's here more often than she's home. I can't see what fun she gets out of running around these hills stripped to the skin carrying your mate on her shoulders."

"I wouldn't know," I said. "Certainly you never seem to enjoy performing that service for me."

"I don't even like the thought of it. I'm not an animal, after all."

"But you are," I said. "So am I. The only difference is that I am a superior animal and you, being inferior, conform to my wishes. It is a law of nature that the superior type will inevitably rule. The inferior either conforms or dies. And you have no desire to die."

He shook his head. "But I can still object," he said.

"At that?" I asked pointing across the meadow with a primary digit.

Edith was running, her long yellow hair floating free behind her. Ven, high on her shoulders in a seat the two of them had contrived, waved gaily at us as they came up. Edith was flushed and laughing. Her eyes sparkled and her smooth bronze body gleamed in the sunlight. She lowered Ven to the ground, slipped the harness off her smooth shoulders and stood behind my mate, breathing deeply but not at all distressed.

"Oh, Donald!" she said. "We had a wonderful climb—clear up to the top of the ridge! And coming down was almost like flying! I'll tell you all about it in a minute, right after I take a dip in the pool. Ven doesn't like it when I sweat." She turned and ran down to the little pool in the meadow.

"See what I mean!" Donald gritted.

"She seems happy. She's not hurt. And Ven's little weight doesn't seem to bother her. What are you complaining about?"

Donald growled something unintelligible, turned on his heel and walked away.

I let him go. There was no sense in making him angrier than he was. After a moment the snarl of his car's engine rose to a crescendo then faded away into the distance.

A few minutes later Edith came back to the ship. "Why did Don leave?" she asked.

"Perhaps he had something to do," Ven said.

She pouted. "He's always so busy nowadays," she said sulkily. "He isn't nice like he used to be. Do you think he's tired of me?"

"No, I don't think so. He just doesn't like you spending so much time up here," I said.

"But it's fun—and Ven likes it," she said. "I like it too. And since he isn't home much any more, it's the only place where I can relax and be myself." She brushed the drops of water from her body and shook out her damp hair. "It's wonderful up here—so quiet and peaceful—and Ven's so nice."

My mate's aura glowed a pleased pink as I turned an embarrassed lavender. It was almost criminal, I thought, what Ven had done to the girl. Donald might be my servant, but I had never attempted to condition him into liking it. As much as possible we operated as equals, rather than in this sickening relationship which Ven had imposed upon Edith. To avoid showing my displeasure I went up to the control room, donned my helmet and went into rapport with Donald.

"I'm sorry," I said. "I hadn't realized the true situation. The best thing for both of us is for Ven and me to leave as quickly as possible."

"How quick is that?" he shot back angrily.

"Four thousand pounds more," I said.

"Whew! That can must drink tin."

"It takes a great deal to leave a planet," I said. "And hyperspace demands a great deal more. Once we develop an inertialess drive it will be easier. But we've only been working on it a thousand years. These things take time."

"I imagine. Well, are you going to do anything about Edith?"

"No," I said. "It would only make things worse. The relationship has gone too far. Ven has become an Authority-image."

"You could break it."

"But I won't. I'm fond of Ven."

"You're a damned little tyrant," Donald said. "You like to see a human squirm."

"Be thankful that I'm the worst tyrant you'll see," I answered sharply. "You could really learn about them if the Slaads knew you existed. They're more advanced than you. And, unlike us, they're warlike and predatory. They breed mammals for food. However, I'll put up a marker on your moon before I leave. They respect Thalassa and won't preempt our claims."

"You mean you're going to lay claim to Earth?"

"Only technically. We'll exercise it only if the Governing Council decides it will be to our advantage."

"What would you do if you took over?" Don asked curiously.

"Clean things up," I said. "Stop wars, stabilize the population, increase production and distribution, give you an effective central government and an understandable legal code, and eliminate the unfit. In three generations you'd be Class VI all over your planet."

"It sounds good. What's the catch."

"The catch," I said, "is that you wouldn't like it. You mammals are erratic, emotional and uncontrolled. You do not reason well, and you have no race discipline."

"What's that?"

"The capability of sacrificing units for the benefit of the whole. Eugenics control, culling the unfit."

"You're talking about human beings!" Donald exploded.

"And what makes a human being different from any other animal?" I asked. "Would you hesitate to dispose of an animal that was unfit to breed?"

He sighed. "No," he said. "But that's not the same."

"What's the difference? And realize, it's done for your betterment."

"Just a bunch of murderous little altruists," Donald sneered. "Out of the kindness of your cold-blooded hearts—"

"That's the trouble with you lower orders," I interrupted. "You get emotional. Your observations have no basis in logic. Actually, the Galaxy wouldn't even quiver if the lot of you disappeared tomorrow. Yet you think the universe rotates about your heads."

"I didn't—"

"Don't interrupt," I snapped. "You—your race—your whole pitiful little civilization is ready mentally and almost ready technologically to commit suicide. If we came and saved you, you would owe us eternal gratitude, but I doubt if we'd get it."

"You wouldn't," Donald assured me. "There wouldn't be a human alive who wouldn't hate you."

"I realize that—and that is one of the reasons I should report your world unfavorably to the council. We could hardly take on an altruism mission like this unless we felt that our work would be appreciated. It would be better to let you kill yourselves."

"Altruism!"

"In a sense. At least your race would be the greater gainers. All we'd get would be your excess population."

"And what would you want them for—slaves?"

"Authority, no!" I said, shocked in spite of myself. "We'd merely process them for food."

He was silent after that.

Donald was away again, at a publisher's meeting. Our new book laid in Restoration England was going to be an even greater success than the first if the advance notices were any criterion. Edith was at a studio party celebrating the completion of the picture in which she was working. And Ven was bored.

For awhile she sat in on Donald's conference in a city called New York, but that proved to be uninteresting. I was busy with a faulty fuel feed in the drive chamber. The sun was hot, and the day was promising to be extremely warm even though it was not yet noon. It was one of those days when nothing happens, and I was grateful for it. I had had enough of emotional tangles to last me for some time. It was almost soothing to work with the robots on insensate machinery rather than supervise a pair of highly charged mammals and a hardly less unstable mate.

The association with these entities hadn't done Ven a great deal of good. In fact, I could notice a deterioration of her character that bothered me. She no longer looked at me with respect. Indeed, her yellow eyes at times held a pitying amusement that I should be so weak as to argue with Donald. I didn't bother to point out that the three tons of power metal had virtually all been brought aboard through Donald's efforts, and that our conveniences, our defenses, our robots and our very lives were due to the working arrangements I had established.

The only useful thing Edith had done in the past month was to help me change the tube liners in the steering jets. Her size and strength had made the job easy—and it was normally a hard one, since the robots didn't have the flexibility or balance that Edith, with her dancer's body, possessed. The job had taken two days. It would have taken better than a week if I had to use robots.

The mammals, I thought, would be of distinct value as members of spaceport maintenance crews. Their combination of immense strength and high intelligence would be useful to our society. I made a note of it and added it to the data I was assembling for the Council. It was foolish, perhaps, but I couldn't help feeling an interest in these creatures.

I looked across the little valley that was our domain. It was an idyllic life we were leading. Unhurried—peaceful—the sort of life I thoroughly enjoyed. It would have been perfect if it wasn't for the insane and dangerous world on which it was being lived.

Of course it was too good to last. Idylls invariably are. The peace of ours was shattered abruptly when Ven came into the drive room and disturbed my work. Her aura blazed a rich violet.

"Eu," she said. "Come up to the control room. Something's wrong!"

"What," I asked.

"It's Edith. I can't do a thing with her."

"You're not supposed to. She's working now."

"She is not! Her studio has finished the picture and they're having a party."

"That's nice. I hope you're letting her have a good time."

"I told her to. But I never imagined what they'd be doing!" Ven's voice was anguished.

"Well, what *are* they doing?"

"Ingesting ethanol to excess!"

"Ethanol!" I gasped. "Oh no!"

I hadn't realized that normal mammals consumed excess amounts of the stuff, although there were references to it in the literature. I thought that was merely literary exaggeration. After all, we had been here scarcely half a year, and we hadn't really learned too much about the details of mammalian society. Donald's kidneys had forced him to lead a quiet life, and the passing of Edith from his control to Ven's had caused no remarkable alterations in her doings.

I should have paid more attention to their customs. But I had been too busy. I swore as I reached for my control helmet. I'd have to stop this before it became serious. Donald would be of no help to me. He was several thousand vursts away, and even under the best circumstances couldn't be expected back for a day.

I didn't bother to call him, but instead adjusted the controls to Edith's setting.

CHAPTER VI

A horde of gaily dressed mammals surrounded me, their faces and bodies oddly fuzzy and distorted. Edith's voice was equally fuzzy. There was something wrong with her centers. I tapped the helmet and checked the controller just in case it was on our end, but they were functioning perfectly. There was nothing wrong—merely the fact that ethanol was disturbing the biocircuits I had implanted in her brain. I swore a few choice expletives of Low Thalassan and tried to get through by increasing the power. It did no good.

"I c'n still feel that li'l lizard in m' head," Edith announced. "Gimme another drink. I wanna wash her out. Darn li'l lizard makes me do things I dowanna do. It wants me to quit, but I wanna get drunk."

"Take it easy," a fuzzy male face said. "You're loaded. Why does a nice chick like you hafta be loaded? Whyncha get outa here? I gotta nice place over in Santa Monica where—"

The face disappeared.

"Hey! Alice! Golly, I almos' din't reckanize you. Howya doin?"

"Better than you, Edith. You're drunk. And from the looks of you, you're going to be sick if you don't get some fresh air."

"Gotta go spit in the eye of my li'l lizard," Edith said. "Y'wanna come with me? I got Don's car. We c'n get outa here an' get some fresh air—an' I c'n tell that li'l lizard what I think of her."

"What are you talking about?"

"You wanna see my li'l lizard. She's got yella eyes, and a li'l tail, and she turns all kindsa colors, and she lives in a rock with a door in it, an she makes me do things I dowanna do. It ain't so bad though. Mosta the time I like it. Not alla time though. That's why I wanna spit in her eye. She c'n tell me all she wants—but she's gotta leave me'n Don alone. I love that guy." Edith started sobbing—why, I couldn't understand.

"She's maudlin," I said to Ven. "No one's going to believe a thing she is saying. But this should be a warning to us. We'll have to put in a block against drinking ethanol. I didn't realize how badly it can affect the biocircuits." I handed the helmet back to Ven. "You can watch this mess if you want to. I'm going to our quarters."

I slipped out of the control chair and walked across the room.

I was stronger now, more accustomed to the gravity, and it didn't bother me unless I had to stand for long periods of time. I turned in the doorway to look at Ven. She had the helmet on again and her aura was a crackling red. I shook my head. Edith was due for a bad time when the effects of that hydrocarbon wore off.

I had hardly fallen into light estivation when Ven's projection crashed through my antennae.

"Eu! Get up! Come here quickly!"

With a groan I came slowly back to full facility and ran to the control room. Ven's face was filled with panic.

"They're coming up here," she said. "A whole carful of them!"

"Who?"

"Edith's drunken friends! Somehow she's collected six of them and they're driving up here to spit in my eye!"

Despite myself, I laughed. Ven looked so outraged I couldn't help it.

"We can close the airlock," I said, "and they can't tell us from a rock."

"I won't! I'm going to teach that girl a lesson she won't forget in a hurry! I've listened to myself being insulted for two hours—and she's still going strong. When she gets up here I'll show her whose eye she'll spit in!"

Ven was raging. I'd never seen her so emotional before. Her aura swelled and ebbed in ruddy shades as her breath came and went in short gasps.

"And how do you propose to do that?" I asked.

"I'll stat her!" Ven raged. "I'll stat every one of them!"

I blinked. "I wouldn't do that," I said mildly. "What can we do with them? The two we have are bad enough. And if you stat them, we'll have to kill or condition them. We couldn't let them go home with a story like the one they'd tell."

"I don't care," Ven said. "You can do what you like about the rest of them, but that Edith is going to learn a lesson." She was being emotional and quite unwilling to listen to reason—and she was larger and stronger than I. Despite my protests, she jerked a stat projector from the rack and strode toward the open airlock.

"Thalassa!" she exclaimed. "They're coming through the gate! They'll be here in a minute."

I could hear the roar of a protesting engine groaning up the trail to the lower meadow as I hurried after Ven. As I reached the airlock, the gray body of Donald's station wagon poked its nose around the trees below our ship.

Ven stood rigidly in the airlock, waiting, her lips tight and her eyes narrow. She took a firmer grip on the stat as the car stopped and the giggling, half-sober humans tumbled out. I was in a quandary. I didn't want Ven to shoot, but I couldn't close the airlock with her inside it. So I stood, hesitating while the group of gaily dressed mammals came toward us through the trees, their high voices loud in the stillness.

"Gotta find that li'l lizard an tell her to stop meddling with my life," Edith's voice came to my ears.

Ven stiffened beside me as the group broke out of the trees in front of the ship.

"Why, Edie, it's beautiful!" a voice said. "It's a fairy glen! No wonder you'd never tell us where you got that suntan! And that big rock—it's just like you said—And—uh!" The voice never finished as Ven pressed the trigger.

I looked down at the six crumpled mammalian bodies and the lone standing figure that looked stupidly up at us.

"Well," I said. "You've done it this time. Now are you satisfied?

"No," Ven said. "Not half." Her voice was tight with anger. She looked down at Edith. "Come here!" she said.

"Dowanna," Edith replied uncertainly. "You've made Don leave me. I don't like you." But habit was stronger than alcohol and under the furious lash of Ven's voice she came unsteadily forward.

"Do you understand me, you little sarf!" Ven snapped icily. "I said *come here*!" She took the control box from her waist and viciously twisted the intensity dial to maximum. At this range its force was irresistible, even with alcohol-deadened synapses. Edith shuddered and moved toward us, her hands clumsily tearing at the fabric that covered her.

"I'm comin'! You don' hafta shout. I ain't deaf. I ain't done nothin'!" She sat down beside the airlock and struggled out of her clothing, ripping the thin fabric under the last of Ven's anger until she was completely naked. Then she stood up and reached her hands toward Ven.

"You're not going to try to ride her while she's in that condition?" I said.

"This is my affair," Ven replied grimly. "I'm going to get this settled."

I shrugged.

There was no sense reasoning with her while she was in that mood. And if she wanted to kill herself that was her concern. I watched her drop onto Edith's shoulders, wind one hand viciously into the mammal's long blonde hair and guide the gross body into a shambling walk toward the meadow. Edith swayed dangerously, but somehow she managed to stay on her feet as they disappeared into the trees.

I walked over to the six bodies, gave each of them a light stat to make sure they would remain quiet and sat down beside the nearest one to think.

Ven's anger had left me a sizeable problem. What on earth could I do with six human females? I needed them like I needed a broken digit. Time passed and the sun rose toward the zenith, and finally I came to a decision. Since we had them on our hands, we might as well make use of them. Killing would be too dangerous.

And presently Edith came through the trees, a sick, tired, sober Edith whose face was dirty and tear streaked, carrying a grim Ven whose aura smoldered a reddish brown.

"What did you do to her?" I asked.

"None of your business," Ven snapped. "She's all right now. Aren't you, Edith?"

"Yes, Ven—and I won't do it again. Honest I won't."

"You'd better not," Ven said grimly. "Now I suppose we have some work to do."

"You certainly have," I said. "If it wasn't for your temper we wouldn't have this mess on our hands. Now get moving! Have Edith carry these girls to the ship." I gestured at the prone bodies. "And you, get inside and bring out the control equipment and connect the leads to the computer." I was angry, too. Under the force of my superior will, the two females scurried to obey. "I'm disgusted with you, Ven," I said angrily. "Just because your pet went to a party, you don't have to act childish. Did you expect she'd behave like a Thalassan?"

"I trusted her," Ven said.

"It just goes to show that you can't trust an animal too far," I said. "Now get moving. Bring the probes first. We have a lot of work to do before evening."

It was finished sooner than I expected. The sun was still in the sky, but close to the edge of the hills. The row of mammalian bodies slumbered peacefully beside the airlock. Ven looked down at them speculatively.

"No," I said. "You have one, and that's enough."

"But," Ven said.

"I've humored you," I said. "I've let you act like a lower order. Now I want to see you behave like a civilized being. For unless you do, I shall have to take steps. I'm tired of this childishness."

"I'll be all right now," Ven replied. "We've come to an understanding." She gestured at Edith with her primary digit and the big mammal shivered. I wondered what Ven had done to her. Edith was thoroughly cowed—actually afraid of little Ven, who was less than one fifth her size. In a way, I felt an odd sort of pride in my mate that she should achieve mastery over such an intelligent and potentially dangerous brute. I knew perfectly well that I'd never dare attempt such dominance over Donald unless I was prepared to rob him of the mentality that made him useful. But I consoled myself with the thought that this female was peculiarly susceptible to domination.

"We'd better get that car out of sight," Ven said. She nodded to Edith. The human obediently trotted off in the direction of the car. A few moments later the sound of the motor rose and fell as she concealed it in the trees.

As soon as I could, I contacted Donald and told him what had happened. Fortunately he was alone, so his exclamation of surprise and consternation didn't arouse any suspicion.

"Ethanol, eh?" he said speculatively.

It was easy to follow the trend of his thoughts. "Don't get any ideas," I warned in my best TV villain manner. "I have Edith up here with me. If you want to see her again, you'd better stay sober."

"I wouldn't think of crossing you," he assured me insincerely. "I'm too close to being rid of you."

"Well—what do we do?" I asked. "You're the expert on this insane society of yours."

"You've done it," he said. "I don't think it was smart of you, but under the circumstances, I can't see how you could have done anything else. I warned you about Ven and Edith," he added—rather gloatingly, I thought. "Now you're in for it." His voice was almost gay.

"How?"

"Six women vanishing all at once is going to cause a stir even in Los Angeles," he said.

"After an ethanol party?" I asked curiously. "Six dancers out of a production that used a hundred? Your city will never miss them."

"But their families will."

Families! I hadn't thought of that. Mammals had strong family ties—probably due to their method of reproduction. We Thalassans, coming as we did from eggs, had none of this. The state incubators and the creches were our only contact with parenthood. We had no families. "Hmm," I said. "I hadn't thought of that."

"Well, you'd better start. I hope it gives you a headache."

"You get nastier every time I talk with you," I complained.

"I have my reasons," he said bitterly. "Now, if you're through with me, little master, I think I'd like to get some sleep. In the meantime you'd better get them back to their homes before they're missed."

"I can't," I confessed. "The controller isn't big enough to handle eight of you—not as individuals."

Donald chuckled grimly. "That's your worry. Remember, unless you find out which of them will be missed and act accordingly, you're going to be very much in the public eye."

I didn't feel too happy as I cut off, but Donald had given me an idea.

One by one I checked the new proxies. Of the six, two were living together. They had the casual emotional involvement with males so characteristic of this species, but they could remain here for several days without causing comment. Of the remaining four, one had a roommate and would be difficult to extract; another was living alone; still another was mated and had an offspring, but she was not living with her mate—a legal action having separated her much as it separates incompatible Thalassans. The offspring, however, was living with her when she wasn't working, a not unusual situation on this world, but one which could have some complications unless she was returned to it very shortly.

The last was living with her parents and was seriously involved emotionally with a male. She was planning to be officially mated in the near future, although it would be legal fiction rather than fact since she was already nurturing a living embryo of some three weeks development. I debated whether to remove it, a simple enough manipulation, but decided against it. It would be interesting to observe a mammalian reproduction. But to remove her from her family and her unofficial mate was a task that might be difficult. I needed help.

I projected a call for Ven, phrasing it imperatively so she could have no doubt about its urgency. Her answer was quick and clear.

"I'm coming," she said.

"Good. I need you. And bring Edith. We have a problem that will require her talents."

"She'll be happy to cooperate." Ven's projection was cheerfully confident.

"You did her no permanent damage, I hope."

"Not a bit. In fact, you'd never know she's been disciplined."

"Well, get in here, both of you. We have work to do."

Edith had trouble squeezing into the control room and, despite her skin conditioning, the place quickly filled with her scent. But Ven and I were old hands now and took it in stride. She grasped the problem instantly. "The only one who might be any trouble is Alice. Her family and her boy friend can be difficult. The others won't need much effort, except for Grace. She'd better be returned to her baby as soon as possible."

"How soon?" I asked.

"The baby isn't living with her," Edith added, "not while she's working, but she sees it regularly. Every day or two, I believe."

I sighed. That solved the biggest problem.

"We had better start at once," Ven said.

I ignored her and looked inquiringly at Edith. "What would you do?" I asked, flashing a cold projection at Ven to stay out of this.

"Well—if I had to do it, I'd send Alice and Grace home. I wouldn't do anything to Alice except block her from talking about this place and what happened. Grace I'd put under full control, have her pick up her baby, go home and pack to leave. As soon as she's ready to go, bring her out here."

"The infant, too?"

"Of course. A baby's no bother."

This, I thought, was something of an understatement.

"And what of the others?" I asked.

"Velma has a nosey roommate. Have her start a fight and leave angry. She hasn't much baggage, and it won't be any trouble for her to collect it. As for the other three, I think Joan's being kept. She can't afford a single apartment on her salary. Loleta and Marian are always out, sometimes for days. Their landlady won't think a thing of it. If they never return, she'll just pack their things and rent the room to someone else. I know that old witch.

I'd just keep those three here and not worry about them. Nobody's going to make any fuss about three chorines disappearing. Later on you can make them write letters enclosing money to send their clothes to another city. Then they can be picked up and stored. That should give us a year before anyone gets suspicious enough to look for them."

"Edith," I said, "you're a genius."

"I got you into this mess," Edith said. "So, perhaps I'd better get you out."

"But your fellow mammals—"

"You haven't hurt me—not much, anyway," Edith said. "So I don't suppose you'll hurt them. And, besides, I don't want Ven mad at me like she was this afternoon. Anyway—you'll be gone soon."

"I think I shall regret leaving," I said honestly. "There is a great deal about you mammals I am beginning to suspect I do not know."

"You aren't kidding," she said with faint bitterness so similar to Donald's that my antennae quivered. "But it's been quite an experience. I'll tell my kids when I have them—but they're not going to believe me."

"I hope you have those children—and raise them to maturity," I said.

The tone of my voice caused her to look at me with sudden fear on her face. But at the sight of my impassive features it died away. "You scared me for a moment," she said.

"Did I? I didn't mean to."

CHAPTER VII

The next week kept us busy following Edith's instructions. I didn't see how they would apply to Alice, but Edith knew her species better than I. Alice's silence and the prying inquisitiveness of her parents and her boyfriend worked like magic. Alice finally became angry and after a stormy scene left the house, swearing never to return. Edith picked her up as she walked away; Ven turned on the control and turned the threat to fact. Later I took a leaf from Edith's book and sent Alice to San Francisco, where I had her write a pair of bitter letters to her parents and her extralegal mate. After that I felt more secure.

The others worked out exactly as Edith predicted. No trouble at all. By the time Donald returned from the East with a ton of tin ingots in a small truck our training schedule was well set up. The robots and I had managed to build a multiplex controller similar to those we used on Thalassa on the state farms, but much smaller. It could handle the proxies en masse or as individuals. While far less sensitive than the one in the ship, it was effective enough for our rather elementary purposes.

Edith, who was running the group under Ven's supervision, had them lined up in a row to greet Donald as he came up the hill toward the ship.

"The place looks like a nudist colony," Donald grumbled. "You haven't improved it any." He eyed the file of mammals trooping down to the truck to unload the tin ingots. "I have another ton lined up for delivery as soon as you get this processed," he said.

"Good," I replied. "We'll leave as soon as it's aboard. I don't like the looks of your recent actions."

"Mine?" I shook my head. "Oh, you mean the world situation." I nodded. "You shouldn't worry about it. You should have seen it this time last year."

I shrugged. I would never really understand these creatures. Their brains functioned differently. "You frighten me with your wild displays of emotion. Someday one of you is going to start something and your world is going to go up in fire."

"I don't think so," he said. "I have some ideas about that. With the money from your stories and with what you have taught me, I think there will be some changes." There was a peculiar expression in his eyes that I couldn't identify. It made me vaguely uneasy. "I've been doing a lot of thinking since you met up with Edie and me. What this world needs is someone who can run it."

"That's obvious," I said. "Until your society catches up with your technology you will be in constant danger. You mammals will have to learn to discipline your emotions."

His face twisted. "I've had a good practical course in that," he said. "Now I'm getting post-graduate training." He gestured at the women coming up the hill carrying the silver tin ingots. "Just how long do you think I can endure something like this?"

"Like what?" I asked.

"Do I have to draw you a diagram?" he asked. "Ever since you lizards came into my life I haven't been able to touch a woman. Not even Edith—and she's my wife. Just how much of this do you think I can take?"

"Oh!" I exclaimed with dawning comprehension. "I think I see."

The situation would have been amusing if it wasn't so stupid. I was surprised that I hadn't realized it before. There was, I knew, a certain amount of feedback in a bipolar control circuit. Obviously enough of Ven's conditioning, and mine, had seeped through to affect Donald and Edith's normal relationships. Mammals were far more preoccupied with sex than we were. Their books, magazines, television and motion pictures reeked of it. It was present in almost every piece of advertising, and four of our six new proxies were living histories of it. Yet Donald and Edith, because of our feedback, had been kept as continent as novitiates for the priesthood of Authority!

"I'm a perfectly normal male," Donald said. "Just what do you think you've been doing to me? I can't drink. I can't make love. I can't do anything except collect tin for you lizards. Just why do you think I hate you? Now you surround me with a whole damned untouchable harem! Are you trying to drive me insane?"

I laughed, and Donald recognize the sound for what it was.

"Oh, *damn* you!" he said bitterly. "How would you like to be married for eight months and for six of them be unable to touch your wife? Just why do you think Edith tried to get drunk? I could kill you cheerfully for what you've done to us!"

"Oh!" I said. There was a world of understanding opening in front of me. Of course, it would do no good to tell him that Ven and I had remained in enforced continence for five years. It was just the Eugenics council working through us—entirely involuntarily. What was bothering Donald and Edith was so absurdly simple that neither Ven nor I would have thought to ask. And the mammals with their peculiar customs and habits would never have told us unless—as had happened—the pressure became too great.

What our mammals needed was a good dose of Va Krul's basic therapy. If Edith were fertilized as a result of it, so much the better. It would keep her attention where it more properly belonged. The thought would never have occurred to me in my present state. Since I was content, I had erroneously assumed that everything was in harmony.

"You might as well go home," I said. "Take Edith with you. We won't need you for several days."

"Why?"

"You'll find things a little different. I'll make a few adjustments on the controller."

To my surprise Don didn't appear happy at all. "Does that mean what I think it does?" he demanded. "Do you think I'll get any satisfaction out of being controlled *even there*?"

"I don't know about the pleasure," I said coldly, "but I do know that it will improve your attitude."

Donald raged at me, his brain white with anger. "So help me God, Eu Kor, someday I'm going to kill you for this! It's the ultimate insult."

"You're not going to do anything," I said calmly. His voice dissolved into obscenity. For a moment I felt sorry for him until I remembered the basic truth that none of us are free—and the most intelligent, naturally, are the least free of all. They are bound by their commitments, their duties, their responsibilities, and by their intelligence itself. If a superior intelligence occasionally exhibits petty lapses—which amuse him or relieve his boredom—it is not the place of the less endowed to construe it as a sign of equality.

Some—like Ven and me—have known their place from birth. Others, like Edith and Alice, learn easily with a minimum amount of pain. Some like Grace learn hard; and some—like Donald—do not learn at all.

Donald was the eternal rebel, complying because he must, yet seething with resentment because he did. He was the personification of drive without innate control, ambition without humility, intelligence without wisdom. As he had been, he was not quite enough. At best he would have been a minor author and a petty domestic tyrant. He would never have been a threat simply because he didn't have the ability or training. But I had given him what he lacked. The knowledge I had impressed upon his mind would give him a tremendous advantage over his fellow mammals, and his tendencies toward domestic tyranny would expand to include others. His glandular attitude would pervert his knowledge to the detriment of humankind. He could become a thing so dangerous that it could destroy this precariously balanced world.

I went into the ship and set up a world matrix on the computer, using all the data I had accumulated, secured the answer, and then inserted Donald's potential into the matrix. I then ordered a probability extrapolation for both matrices, equating the solutions with survival.

The answers confirmed my thoughts. With the matrix as it stood, the twenty year survival prediction was 65 per cent, which wasn't too bad since few advanced-technology worlds have better than an 85 per cent survival probability. But with Donald in the matrix, the survival prediction was zero!

I knew what I must do. I could not leave him behind as I had planned. Nor could I inflict the senseless cruelty of brainblotting. He would have to be mercifully destroyed.

Although I was fond of Donald, and his death would leave me sick for weeks, it would not be right to let my creation live and condemn the mammal race to death. I could not exterminate a race Authority had created.

The guilt syndrome would be shattering. Of course, if they killed each other that was not my concern.

But until we left I would give him all the freedom he could use. Outside of the minimum of control, he would be free to do and act as he pleased. I didn't owe it to him, yet it was not his fault that he had come into my hands. And when I returned to Thalassa I would tell the Council what I had done and ask for justice. Perhaps we could save this world from itself even as we had saved others. The question of gratitude would be immaterial.

With a firm hand to set them on the track, the mammals might learn the values of intelligence and cooperation before it was too late. They might understand the realities of existence rather than fall victim to their glandular fancies. They might. But if they did, one thing would be certain—they would learn it the hard way. Donald was proof of that.

I went to our living quarters, and presently Ven joined me. "They're all in for the night, Eu," she said.

"That's good. How are they coming along?"

"Splendidly. Another week should see the end of the training. Edith was a good experience for me in handling these. I'm not making the mistakes I did. I'm finding the blocks and removing them. One of them, the one called Grace, should be even better than Edith."

"As a mount?" I asked with faint humor. "Or as a working proxy?"

"Both," Ven said promptly. "She's stronger and more intelligent. Yet even so I think I shall always like Edith best."

"One's first dependent is always one's fondest memory," I replied sententiously, "But you'll forget them all when we're back on Thalassa."

"I won't," Ven said. "I'll never forget Edith."

"Never is a long time," I said gently. "I shall even forget the pain of killing Donald some day."

"Then you've decided to eliminate him?" Ven said.

I nodded. "It's necessary," I said. "This world wouldn't be safe with him alive."

"Poor Edith. She's fond of the brute," Ven said. She moved toward the doorway.

"Where are you going?" I asked.

"I want to talk to Edith. Perhaps I can prepare her."

"No. Don't," I said. "Contact her if you wish, but tell her nothing."

"Very well," she said. I smiled as she disappeared. Ven was going to miss her pet once we had left. It was obvious.

"Eu! Quick!" Ven's projection crackled in my brain. "They're fighting! Edith's being hurt, and I can't touch them! They've set up a block!"

I ran for the control room, slapped the helmet on my head, reached for the controls—and stopped, laughing.

"Stop them!" Ven screamed. Her aura blazed a brilliant white and her projection nearly knocked me down. She reached for the control switch, but I slapped her hand away.

"Quiet!" I snapped. "They're not fighting, you little fool! Turn on your audio and listen and stop acting silly!"

Ven did as I told her and her aura changed to a fiery pink. "Oh!" she said in a small voice, "but they never—"

I must have made some mistake in revising the controllers—or feedback was stronger than I suspected—for the Va Krul syndrome came back along our lines of contact with explosive force! Desperately I reached for the switch—but my hand froze in midair as an intolerable wave of emotion drove Ven and me together like two pieces of iron with opposite magnetic charge! The last thing I remember was being enveloped in the flaring golden glow of Ven's aura.

I came to my senses in our living quarters. I was stunned—exhausted—limp and gasping.

"Thalassa!" I said weakly, "we've *really* done it now!"

Ven smiled a pale blue radiance at me. "You have become strong, living on this heavy world," she said. "I like it."

"But—but!" I sputtered. "It was so—it can't—it couldn't—"

"But it did," Ven said softly. "And I'm glad it did."

"I don't mean that. What I mean to say was that it was so—"

"Unexpected?"

"No! So utterly—"

"Satisfying?" she asked.

"Stop interrupting! It was all of that and more. But what I want to say is that we've violated the prime restriction for space travellers. How could we do it?"

"You're forgetting that for some time we have been living upon this emotion-charged world," Ven said. "The steady erosion was more than our conditioning could take. The feedback was merely the last in a whole series of disruptive stimuli. It was the trigger, but our defenses had been weakened long before. Not that I'm sorry," she added quickly. "For weeks I've been wondering what sort of a mate you'd be when this trip was over. I'm not unhappy with the preview." She smiled at me and the whole of our living quarters was filled with a bright tender blue.

"The natives," I said worriedly. "We were in contact with them."

Ven's aura darkened. "I had forgotten them," she said. "I hope that the feedback wasn't intensified and returned to them. I'd better look." She started for the control room and I followed more slowly.

"There's no damage," she said from beneath the helmet. "Edith feels just as I do."

I took my helmet and coded Don's pattern on the selector. Peculiar, I thought with vague wonder. Most peculiar. For the first time Donald and I were in true rapport. His mind was slow, lazy, sluggish—even his ambition was sated for the moment. Could it be, I wondered, that we could find agreement through our *emotions*? Was it frustration that drove him? Whatever the block had been it was gone now. This was a true empathic meeting—something far more satisfying than our previous conflict.

I relaxed in it, feeling the slow langorous questings of his mind even as he felt mine. There was a sense of brotherhood that transcended differences in race and culture. We were down to basics, on the oldest meeting ground of life.

He was wondering idly what the outcome of this might be—conscious of me, but careless. It jolted me. He might be uncertain, but I *knew* Ven was from good family stock, and "good" to a Thalassan meant something entirely different than it commonly did to the natives of this planet!

I disengaged hurriedly and shook Ven out of her rapport with Edith. "We've no time to lose," I said. "We must leave at once! You know what's going to happen!"

"I know," Ven said. "I feel the changes already."

"That's just in your mind," I snapped.

"We're not going home," she said. There was a note of prophecy in her voice. "We'll never make it."

"We can't stay here!"

"I know."

"Then what are we going to do?"

We couldn't stay here. But we couldn't go home either. The trip would take weeks, and hyperspace is fatal to a gravid Thalassan female. That was something we learned long ago, and the principal reason for continence-conditioning for couples in space. What was more, I knew that where Ven stayed, I would stay.

"Remember the fourth planet of this system?" Ven asked.

"Yes. Ideal gravity, adequate oxygen, but too cold."

"And with no intelligent life," Ven added. "That's an advantage—and we can beat the cold. It wouldn't be too hard to build domes. We have plenty of power metal, and a matricizer. We could hatch our clutch there. With the mammals to help us, we should be able to make a comfortable enough life for the forty years it'll take to bring our offspring to maturity. We should be able to do this easily, and still get home before we're strangers."

"Hmm," I said. "It's possible. And we can use this world for a supply base. But would you care to live on that cold barren planet?"

"There are worse places," she said matter-of-factly. "And we'd be close to everything we'd need."

It did have possibilities. And the mammals could be adapted. They were a more advanced evolutionary form than we, but lower on the adaptive scale—nonspecialized—more so than any other intelligent race I had encountered.

Ven said, "We would actually be doing their race a favor, if the computation of this world's future is correct. Some of them would still survive if this planet commits suicide. And if the prediction is wrong, we would have done no harm. If they reach space, they'll merely find that they've already arrived when they reach the fourth planet."

"Which might be something of a surprise to their explorers," I said with a chuckle. "All right. We'll play it your way."

I was pretty sure how Donald would take this. He was going to be furious, but after all one doesn't make a pet of a wolf and then turn it loose. It's too hard on the livestock. But I didn't think he'd be too unhappy. He'd be the principal human on Mars; and after we left he'd be ruler of a world. And in the meantime he could be a domestic tyrant.

It was fortunate, I thought with a smile, that mammals were essentially polygamous. Donald would make some nasty comments about being a herd sire—but I didn't think his comments would be too sincere. After all, it's not every man that has a chance to become a founding father.

I was still smiling as I turned the dials on the controller and flipped the switch. Founding father—the title was as much mine as his!